ThoughtWorks

Imaginative Problem-Solving Activities for Small Groups

Stephen A. Sadow

Deborah Maas

Frederick Maas

Cottonwood Press, Inc.
Fort Collins, Colorado

Copyright © 1998 by Cottonwood Press, Inc.

Permission is granted to reproduce activities in this book, in other than electronic form, for the purchaser's own personal use in the classroom, provided that the copyright notice appears on each reproduction. Otherwise, no part of this work may be reproduced or transmitted in any form or by any means without written permission from Cottonwood Press.

Requests for permission should be addressed to:

Cottonwood Press
305 West Magnolia, Suite 398
Fort Collins, CO 80521

ISBN 1-877673-33-1

Printed in the United States of America

Cover design by Aaron Nabaum

To Norma,
one of the most creative teachers ever

Table of Contents

About *ThoughtWorks* 5
Using *ThoughtWorks* 7

To Use with Every Activity
   Group Roles 13
   Closure Discussion 14

ThoughtWorks Activities
   Emergency! Emergency! 17
   House Beautiful 21
   On the Road Again 25
   How Does Your Garden Grow? 29
   Wrong Turn 33
   For He's a Jolly Good Fellow 37
   Missing! 41
   My Hero 45
   Welcome Mat 49
   Games People Play 53
   Myth Maker 57
   It's the Law 61
   Time Marches On 65
   Play Ball! 69
   Something Special 73
   The Play Is the Thing 77
   A Place of Our Own 81
   Total Loss 85
   Fit for a King 89
   Statuesque 93

About *ThoughtWorks*

The activities in *ThoughtWorks* are designed to help students learn to work together effectively to solve problems. They promote teamwork, creative thinking and decision making. The activities, which can generally be completed in one to two class periods, can be used to supplement nearly any curriculum, grades 5–9.

With each *ThoughtWorks* activity, students are given a problem to solve or a job to complete during a specified period of time. The task may be tied to reality (as in a call to 9-1-1) or to the world of make believe (as in a group traveling in outer space). Students must persuade, analyze, gather and interpret data in order to solve the problem. They use analytical skills that include forming appropriate questions and testing the validity of what is presented to them.

The plan for each activity is tightly structured, but the results can be highly creative and rich in surprises. We hope that your students will enjoy the challenge of solving the problems presented in *ThoughtWorks*.

Stephen A. Sadow, Ph.D.
Department of Modern Languages
Northeastern University
Boston, MA

Deborah Maas
(elementary language arts)
César Chavez Elementary School
Santa Fe, NM

Fred Maas
(math/science)
Santa Fe Preparatory School
Santa Fe, NM

Using *ThoughtWorks*

1. To begin any activity in *ThoughtWorks*, present the problem situation to the students. You can simply explain the problem, or you can make an overhead transparency or a handout of the problem statement page that starts each activity.

2. Have the class brainstorm questions that will need to be answered in order to solve the problem. Students should *not* start solving the problem yet. They should simply examine the problem by exploring different questions.

    For example, if students were trying to decide what school supplies they should buy with a budget of $25.00 each, they might look at questions like these: What supplies are required by various teachers? What supplies can be reused from last year? Are there any supplies that could be borrowed from someone else? What items are most important to me to have in order to do a good job? If I don't have enough money now, are there items I could buy at a later time? If I can't have everything, how would I rank the things I need in order of importance?

    As students brainstorm, write down all of the questions on the chalkboard or on an overhead transparency.

3. Divide the class into small groups of four or five students each. Explain that everyone in a group has a specific role: *leader, scribe, presenter* or *participant*. To remind students of these roles, you might want to make an overhead transparency or photocopies of the box on page 13. It is a good idea to vary the groups with each activity and to give individual students different roles each time. You might even want to make notes about who has been assigned what roles, for it is easy to forget when you are dealing with a whole class or with a number of classes.

    After students are in groups, explain that their first task is to decide which questions from the brainstormed list are most important to answer in order to solve the problem. Give them a guideline about the number of questions. Some suggested numbers are noted in the teacher instructions for each activity, but you may want to vary these, according to the age and skill level of your group. A minimum of five questions is usually about right.

4. The next task is for students to answer the questions they have selected. Because the problem situation they have been given is fictitious, their answers will be fictitious as well. However, it is important to stress that these answers should be realistic, given the situation as outlined.

5. Based on the answers to the questions, the students should then complete the activity, thus solving the problem as stated. With most of the activities, students must *do* something to solve the problem — create a list, write a play, prepare a budget, etc.

(continued)

(continued)

6. The last step in the activity is to have the groups report to the class. The presenter from each group reports on the questions the group decided to answer, tells the answers and presents (either alone or with the help of other group members) the results of the group's work.

7. After each activity is a page of ideas for "Related Activities." These ideas are helpful to use when some groups finish earlier than others. By going on to a related activity, students will be spending their time in a positive way while waiting for others to finish.

After each activity, have the groups take a look at how well the members worked together. Use the "Closure" questions from page 14 to help them evaluate themselves. (Make an overhead transparency of the questions, or photocopy them for each group.) To monitor how the groups improve over the course of the year, keep track of student responses on a chart or in a notebook.

After your classes complete just a few *ThoughtWorks* activities, both you and the students themselves should see an improvement in teamwork, responsibility and effectiveness at problem-solving in a group situation.

To Use with Every Activity

When completing activities in *ThoughtWorks*, students should be able to refer to the information from "Group Roles," page 13. Photocopy the page for each group, make it into an overhead transparency or summarize the information on a chart.

At the end of every *ThoughtWorks* activity, have students discuss the closure questions on page 14. Note their responses on a chart or journal to be reviewed the next time a *ThoughtWorks* activity is used in class. Students can then monitor their progress during the school year.

Group Roles

Everyone in each group has an assigned role, and everyone has a responsibility to participate. The roles are:

- **Leader.** The leader is responsible for keeping the group on task, making sure all members participate and keeping track of time.

- **Scribe.** The scribe is responsible for writing down questions used and answers given, and for making any necessary charts or diagrams.

- **Presenter.** The presenter is responsible for explaining the group's activity during the reporting session.

- **Participant.** All participants have a responsibility to take part in the activity in a positive way.

Closure Discussion

1. What was difficult about this activity?

2. What did you like best?

3. What was hardest about working in your group?

4. What did you like best about working in your group?

5. How did you make decisions?

6. How would you change this activity next time?

7. How should we create our groups next time?

ThoughtWorks Activities

Emergency! Emergency!
Calling 9-1-1

The problem to solve:

Help! There is a serious emergency in this building, and you and your group are the only people who know about it. Fortunately, there is a phone nearby and you can call 9-1-1. With others in your group, think about what you need to say to the operator who answers your call. Which details of the emergency should you tell the person who answers? Write a script of what to say when you dial 9-1-1 and

Teacher Instructions

Emergency! Emergency!
Calling 9-1-1

With "Emergency! Emergency!" students decide what to tell a 9-1-1 operator when reporting a specific emergency. They solve the problem of deciding what details are most important to include.

Getting started

- Organize the class into groups of three to five students each. Assign the roles of *leader, scribe, presenter* and *participant*. (See box on next page.)
- Go over the problem on page 17 with the class. You may reproduce the situation as a handout or overhead transparency, or you may present it orally to the class.

Creating questions

Supervise as the class brainstorms a list of questions. Ask, "What questions need to be answered in order to provide information to the 9-1-1-operator?" Write the suggested questions on an overhead transparency or on the chalkboard. You may want to direct students to some of the support questions below.

Support questions:

- What is the emergency?
- How many people are involved?
- Where is this emergency taking place?
- How many people will be needed to rescue the victims?
- What experts will be needed?
- How is emergency communication different from normal conversation?

Answering the questions

In their small groups, have students decide which questions they think need to be answered in order to decide what should be included in their script for a 9-1-1 call. Set the minimum number of questions (five or more) at a level suited to the class. Also set a time limit for this portion of the activity. Thirty minutes is usually about right.

After the students decide on the questions, they should write answers to them. Remind students that while the answers are fictitious, they must be realistic and appropriate for a real emergency.

Copyright © 1998 Cottonwood Press, Inc. • 305 West Magnolia, Suite 398 • Fort Collins, Colorado 80521

Teacher Instructions continued

Writing the script

Have students write the script for a 9-1-1 telephone call. You may want to first talk about succinct communication and what makes emergency communication different from normal conversation.

During the activity

While students are working on their answers to the questions, move from group to group, making sure that all students remain active during the work time. Review the specific responsibilities of each group member the first time you check in with a group. At other check-ins, encourage students to consider the following:

- Is everyone getting a chance to talk?
- How will this question help you make decisions about your phone call?
- Are you keeping track of the time? We have _____ minutes left.
- How will you begin the conversation with the 9-1-1 operator?
- What danger are you in as you report this emergency? Will that affect your call?

Reporting

When the allotted time has passed, gather all the groups together again and have the presenters report to the class. The report from each group should include the questions selected and the answers given. With the group member he or she has selected, the presenter for each group should also read the 9-1-1 script aloud to the class. If desired, the rest of the class may also ask questions, which any member of the reporting group may answer.

Assessing the activity

At the completion of the activity, use the "Closure Discussion" handout on page 14 to have students monitor their progress at working in small groups to solve problems.

Group Roles

Everyone in each group has an assigned role, and everyone has a responsibility to participate. The roles are:

- **Leader.** The leader is responsible for keeping the group on task, making sure all members participate and keeping track of time.

- **Scribe.** The scribe is responsible for writing down questions used and answers given, and for making any necessary charts or diagrams.

- **Presenter.** The presenter is responsible for explaining the group's activity during the reporting session.

- **Participant.** All participants have a responsibility to take part in the activity in a positive way.

Copyright © 1998 Cottonwood Press, Inc. • 305 West Magnolia, Suite 398 • Fort Collins, Colorado 80521

Emergency! Emergency!
Related Activities

Social studies

- Have students make a map of the area of their emergency, including any possible escape routes.
- Have students research and report on a recent emergency or disaster situation that occurred in another part of the world.
- Have students research and report on a disaster or emergency in history. Ask them to compare the ability to handle it then with resources available today.

English

- Have students write the script of a radio news broadcast about the emergency.
- Have students write the script for a video teaching others how to use 9-1-1.

General

- Have students create a disaster plan for their school.
- Have students prepare and present an exhibit about using 9-1-1 for students in lower grades.
- Have students prepare a series of posters showing the dos and don'ts of calling 9-1-1.
- Invite a firefighter, police officer or paramedic to class to discuss emergency preparedness in your city.
- Take a field trip to a local police station for a presentation about its 9-1-1 program, or have a 9-1-1 operator come and talk to the class about his or her job.

Science

- Have students find out what types of natural disasters are likely to occur in your area. What makes your area more susceptible to certain disasters?

House Beautiful

Decorating a Home

The problem to solve:

Mr. and Mrs. Sandoval are redecorating their home, and they have chosen your group to create an exciting new design for their two children's bedrooms. Before they will let you begin your work, though, they insist on having a sketch of each room, showing what you plan to do to it.

Draw sketches of both Darren's room and Melissa's room. Show where each piece of furniture will be placed, how you will decorate the walls and what colors you will use.

Teacher Instructions

House Beautiful
Decorating a Home

"House Beautiful" requires students to solve a problem that might be encountered by an interior decorator. They must decide how to redecorate the bedrooms of two children.

Getting started

- Organize the class into groups of three to five students each. Assign the roles of *leader, scribe, presenter* and *participant*. (See box on next page.)

- Briefly discuss the profession of interior decorating with your students. You may want to have magazines such as *Better Homes and Gardens* available as resources.

- Go over the problem on page 21 with the class. You may reproduce the situation as a handout or overhead transparency, or you may present it orally to the class.

Creating questions

Supervise as the class brainstorms a list of questions. Ask, "What questions need to be answered to design the rooms?" Write the suggested questions on an overhead transparency or on the chalkboard. You may want to direct students to some of the support questions below.

Support questions:

- How old are Darren and Melissa?
- How large are their bedrooms?
- What is the architectural style of the house?
- What are some of the kids' special interests?
- What furniture do they already have that they want to use?
- Where are the windows and doors located?

Answering the questions

In their small groups, have students decide which questions they think need to be answered in order to design the rooms. Set the minimum number of questions (five or more) at a level suited to the class. Also set a time limit for this portion of the activity. Thirty minutes is usually about right.

After the students decide on the questions, they should write answers to them. Remind students that while the answers are fictitious, they must be realistic and appropriate for the assignment.

Copyright © 1998 Cottonwood Press, Inc. • 305 West Magnolia, Suite 398 • Fort Collins, Colorado 80521

Teacher Instructions continued

Designing the rooms

Have students plan the rooms and draw a sketch of each.

During the activity

While students are working on their answers to the questions, move from group to group, making sure that all students remain active during the work time. Review the specific responsibilities of each group member the first time you check in with a group. At other check-ins, encourage students to consider the following:

- Is everyone getting a chance to talk?
- How will this question help you make design decisions?
- Are you keeping track of the time? We have _____ minutes left.
- Why have you chosen these colors?
- Why would someone want this in his or her room?
- Do your sketches show all parts of the room?
- Do you think Mr. and Mrs. Sandoval would agree to this design?

Reporting

When the allotted time has passed, gather all the groups together again and have the presenters report to the class. The report from each group should include the questions selected, the answers given and the room designs. The sketches of each room may be displayed by the presenter alone or with the help of other group members. If desired, the rest of the class may ask questions, which any member of the reporting group may answer.

Assessing the activity

At the completion of the activity, use the "Closure Discussion" handout on page 14 to have students monitor their progress at working in small groups to solve problems.

Group Roles

Everyone in each group has an assigned role, and everyone has a responsibility to participate. The roles are:

- **Leader.** The leader is responsible for keeping the group on task, making sure all members participate and keeping track of time.

- **Scribe.** The scribe is responsible for writing down questions used and answers given, and for making any necessary charts or diagrams.

- **Presenter.** The presenter is responsible for explaining the group's activity during the reporting session.

- **Participant.** All participants have a responsibility to take part in the activity in a positive way.

House Beautiful
Related Activities

English

- Have students write a letter to the Sandovals, "selling" them on the new room designs.

Social studies

- Have students research and report on famous restoration projects such as Catherine's Summer Palace near St. Petersburg, Russia, or the renovation of the White House during the Kennedy administration.

Math

- Have students make a shopping list of materials needed to redecorate the rooms as their group suggested. Have them contact local stores and subcontractors to determine costs. Ask them to prepare a budget and write a bid for the job, reminding them to include charges for their time.
- Have students figure out the dimensions of the room and diagram furniture for the room, to scale.

General

- Have students design an ideal room for themselves, making a shoebox diorama of it.
- Invite an interior decorator to visit the class to show his or her portfolio and discuss common design problems and ways to deal with them.
- Have students create a design for a room somewhere other than in a home — for example, in a store, restaurant, mall, pool, amusement park, gymnasium, nursing home or health club.

On the Road Again
Packing Lightly for a Trip

The problem to solve:

Lucky you! Your parents have agreed to let you take an exciting trip to a place you have never been before. You and your group must leave tomorrow. However, room for luggage is extremely limited. Other than a change of clothing for each traveler, the group as a whole can take only eight other items on the trip. Each item must be useful. What eight items will your group bring on the trip?

Teacher Instructions

On the Road Again
Packing Lightly for a Trip

With "On the Road Again," students must solve the problem of what to take on a trip when they have little time to pack and limited space for luggage. Each small group must decide on eight and only eight items to pack for the entire group, in addition to one change of clothing for everyone.

Getting started

- Organize the class into groups of three to five students each. Assign the roles of *leader, scribe, presenter* and *participant*. (See box on next page.)
- Go over the problem on page 25 with the class. You may reproduce the situation as a handout or overhead transparency, or you may present it orally to the class.

Creating questions

Supervise as the class brainstorms a list of questions. Ask, "What questions need to be answered to decide what eight items you will take on this trip?" Write the suggested questions on an overhead transparency or on the chalkboard. You may want to direct students to some of the support questions below.

Support questions:

- Where are we going?
- How long will we be gone?
- What kind of transportation will we use?
- Are there any size limitations?
- Will other groups be joining us?
- Is this a pleasure trip or a working vacation?

Answering the questions

In their small groups, have students decide which questions they think need to be answered in order to decide what eight items to take. Set the minimum number of questions (five or more) at a level suited to the class. Also set a time limit for this portion of the activity. Thirty minutes is usually about right.

After the students decide on the questions, they should write answers to them. Remind students that while the answers are fictitious, they must be realistic and appropriate for the assignment.

Copyright © 1998 Cottonwood Press, Inc. • 305 West Magnolia, Suite 398 • Fort Collins, Colorado 80521

Teacher Instructions continued

Writing the lists

Have students decide on the eight items to take on their trip.

During the activity

While students are working on their answers to the questions, move from group to group, making sure that all students remain active during the work time. Review the specific responsibilities of each group member the first time you check in with a group. At other check-ins, encourage students to consider the following:

- Is everyone getting a chance to talk?
- How will this question help you decide what to bring?
- Are you keeping track of the time? We have _____ minutes left.
- Why is this item a good one to include?
- How will you get this item on such short notice?
- Does everyone in your group agree that this item should be included?

Reporting

When the allotted time has passed, gather all the groups together again and have the presenters report to the class. The report from each group should include the questions selected, the answers given and the list of items. If desired, the rest of the class may also ask questions, which any member of the reporting group may answer.

Assessing the activity

At the completion of the activity, use the "Closure Discussion" handout on page 14 to have students monitor their progress at working in small groups to solve problems.

Group Roles

Everyone in each group has an assigned role, and everyone has a responsibility to participate. The roles are:

- **Leader.** The leader is responsible for keeping the group on task, making sure all members participate and keeping track of time.

- **Scribe.** The scribe is responsible for writing down questions used and answers given, and for making any necessary charts or diagrams.

- **Presenter.** The presenter is responsible for explaining the group's activity during the reporting session.

- **Participant.** All participants have a responsibility to take part in the activity in a positive way.

On the Road Again
Related Activities

Social studies

- Have students research and report on items taken on famous journeys such as Amundsen's voyage to the South Pole, the 1803 Lewis and Clark expedition or American pioneers traveling west in covered wagons.
- Discuss when and why people have to leave in a hurry. Ask students to find some historical examples of such situations.

English

- Have students write a letter to the chamber of commerce of a city they want to visit some day. Have them request brochures on the area's attractions.
- Have students think of one famous person, living or dead, whom they would like to have with them on this trip. Ask them to write about this person and why they would want to have him or her along.
- Have students write a fictitious journal about their travels.

Geography and math

- Have students use a map to plot a trip, including destinations, schedules and realistic travel routes. Have them determine the number of miles they will travel, how much gas they will need and approximately how much it will cost.

General

- Have students produce a brochure advertising their destination.
- Invite a travel agent to class to discuss travel tips.
- Have students draw a picture of one of their "experiences" on the imaginary trip.

How Does Your Garden Grow?
Planning a Garden

The problem to solve:

An environmental group called Gardens, Inc. has offered to supply seeds, seedlings and gardening tools to any class that will plant and raise a vegetable and flower garden on school grounds. You and your group have been asked to plan the garden. Your plan will serve as a model for the entire school.

First, find a place for the garden. It may be outside on school property or inside in boxes and trays. Second, select plants that will grow well where the garden is located. Finally, diagram the garden, showing where you will plant each vegetable and flower.

Teacher Instructions

How Does Your Garden Grow?
Planning a Garden

"How Does Your Garden Grow?" requires students to solve problems that might be encountered when planning a garden. Small groups must decide on a place for a garden on school grounds, select plants and diagram a final plan for the layout of the garden.

Getting started

- Organize the class into groups of three to five students each. Assign the roles of *leader, scribe, presenter* and *participant*. (See box on next page.)
- Go over the problem on page 29 with the class. You may reproduce the situation as a handout or overhead transparency, or you may present it orally to the class.

Creating questions

Supervise as the class brainstorms a list of questions. Ask, "What questions need to be answered in order to plan a garden?" Write the suggested questions on an overhead transparency or on the chalkboard. You may want to direct students to some of the support questions below.

Support questions:

- Where will we plant the garden?
- How long is the growing season in our area?
- What kinds of vegetables and flowers grow well here?
- How much help is available for caring for the garden?
- What tools are available?
- What size will the plants reach?
- If the garden is indoors, what kind of plants grow best in the light and temperature of the area you have selected?

Answering the questions

In their small groups, have students decide which questions they think need to be answered in order to decide how to plan their garden. Set the minimum number of questions (five or more) at a level suited to the class. Also set a time limit for this portion of the activity. Thirty minutes is usually about right.

After the students decide on the questions, they should write answers to them. Remind students that while the answers are fictitious, they must be realistic and appropriate for the assignment.

Copyright © 1998 Cottonwood Press, Inc. • 305 West Magnolia, Suite 398 • Fort Collins, Colorado 80521

Teacher Instructions continued

Planning the garden

Have students plan their gardens.

During the activity

While students are working on their answers to the questions, move from group to group, making sure that all students remain active during the work time. Review the specific responsibilities of each group member the first time you check in with a group. At other check-ins, encourage students to consider the following:

- Is everyone getting a chance to talk?
- How will this question help you decide what to plant?
- Are you keeping track of the time? We have _____ minutes left.
- Is this a practical place to set up a garden?
- What resources does the school have that will help maintain this garden?
- How will the garden be cared for during the summer?

Reporting

When the allotted time has passed, gather all the groups together again and have the presenters report to the class. The report from each group should include the questions selected, the answers given and the diagram of the garden. If desired, the rest of the class can ask questions, which any member of the reporting group may answer.

Assessing the activity

At the completion of the activity, use the "Closure Discussion" handout on page 14 to have students monitor their progress at working in small groups to solve problems.

Group Roles

Everyone in each group has an assigned role, and everyone has a responsibility to participate. The roles are:

- **Leader.** The leader is responsible for keeping the group on task, making sure all members participate and keeping track of time.

- **Scribe.** The scribe is responsible for writing down questions used and answers given, and for making any necessary charts or diagrams.

- **Presenter.** The presenter is responsible for explaining the group's activity during the reporting session.

- **Participant.** All participants have a responsibility to take part in the activity in a positive way.

Copyright © 1998 Cottonwood Press, Inc. • 305 West Magnolia, Suite 398 • Fort Collins, Colorado 80521

How Does Your Garden Grow?
Related Activities

English

- Ask students to imagine that their group's garden is part of a tour of gardens in their city. Have them write a script to use while guiding visitors through the garden.
- Ask students to imagine being a tiny elf or gnome living in the garden. Have them write a story about their life there.
- Have students research pesticides and write both sides of a debate about their use.

Science

- Have students research the climate and growing conditions in another part of the country. Have them plan a garden for that location.
- Have students research and report on famous names in botany and horticulture, like Gregor Mendel, Luther Burbank or George Washington Carver.
- Have students research one of the plants they selected for their garden. Ask them to draw a diagram of the mature plant and label the parts.
- Take a field trip to a local nursery or botanical gardens.
- Have students research and report on different types of gardening, such as hydroponic gardening and organic gardening.

Art

- Have students research and report on artists who specialized in gardens and landscapes, like Claude Monet and Ansel Adams.
- Have students imagine that they can sell seeds from the plants in their garden. Have them design the seed packets for different plants.

General

- Have each group make a model of its garden.
- Have students name their group's garden and then create a logo for marketing and selling the flowers and vegetables.
- Have students plan a vegetarian breakfast, lunch or dinner using only the plants from the class garden.

Wrong Turn
Surviving in Difficult Circumstances

The problem to solve:

Uh-oh. Your little day-hike is turning into a disaster. Those clouds look like they're about to burst, and isn't that the same pond you passed an hour ago? You must be going in circles. You must be lost! It's getting too dark to keep walking, but all you have in your packs are matches, knives, jackets, water and a little food left over from lunch.

You have got to organize yourselves and plan how to proceed. How will you get through the night? How will you find your way home tomorrow?

Teacher Instructions

Wrong Turn
Surviving in Difficult Circumstances

With "Wrong Turn," students solve a problem that might be encountered by a group lost in the woods. Students must decide on a plan for spending the night safely and then finding their way out of the woods.

Getting started

- Organize the class into groups of three to five students each. Assign the roles of *leader, scribe, presenter* and *participant*. (See box on next page.)
- Go over the problem on page 33 with the class. You may reproduce the situation as a handout or overhead transparency, or you may present it orally to the class.

Creating questions

Supervise as the class brainstorms a list of questions. Ask, "What questions need to be answered in order to figure out how to spend the night safely and then find your way out of the woods?" Write the suggested questions on an overhead transparency or on the chalkboard. You may want to direct students to some of the support questions below.

Support questions:

- How many people are in our group?
- What is the temperature likely to be overnight?
- How can we supplement the small amount of food that we have?
- What will we use for shelter tonight?
- How can we signal for help?
- What can we do tomorrow to find our way home?

Answering the questions

In their small groups, have students decide which questions they think need to be answered in order to spend the night safely and find their way out of the woods. Set the minimum number of questions (five or more) at a level suited to the class. Also set a time limit for this portion of the activity. Thirty minutes is usually about right.

After the students decide on the questions, they should write answers to them. Remind students that while the answers are fictitious, they must be realistic and appropriate for the assignment.

Teacher Instructions continued

Making a plan

Have students write their plans for spending the night safely and then finding their way out of the woods.

During the activity

While students are working on their answers to the questions, move from group to group, making sure that all students remain active during the work time. Review the specific responsibilities of each group member the first time you check in with a group. At other check-ins, encourage students to consider the following:

- Is everyone getting a chance to talk?
- How will this question help you decide what to do?
- What is the first decision your group must make?
- Are you keeping track of the time? We have _____ minutes left.
- Who is organizing the group? Why?
- What skills do group members have that will help solve this problem?

Reporting

When the allotted time has passed, gather all the groups together again and have the presenters report to the class. The report from each group should include the questions selected, the answers given and the plan decided upon by the group. If desired, the rest of the class may ask questions, which any member of the reporting group may answer.

Assessing the activity

At the completion of the activity, use the "Closure Discussion" handout on page 14 to have students monitor their progress at working in small groups to solve problems.

Group Roles

Everyone in each group has an assigned role, and everyone has a responsibility to participate. The roles are:

- **Leader.** The leader is responsible for keeping the group on task, making sure all members participate and keeping track of time.

- **Scribe.** The scribe is responsible for writing down questions used and answers given, and for making any necessary charts or diagrams.

- **Presenter.** The presenter is responsible for explaining the group's activity during the reporting session.

- **Participant.** All participants have a responsibility to take part in the activity in a positive way.

Copyright © 1998 Cottonwood Press, Inc. • 305 West Magnolia, Suite 398 • Fort Collins, Colorado 80521

Wrong Turn
Related Activities

English

- Have students research and report on a famous rescue of people from a wilderness area.
- Have students write about their survival plans for a night lost in a large city instead of in the wilderness.
- Have students research and report on equipment used in search and rescue operations.
- Have students imagine that they have been rescued and are met by a reporter. Ask them to write a script of their first conversation with the reporter.
- Have students read aloud and discuss Jack London's short story, "To Build a Fire," or another story about trying to survive in the wilderness.
- Have students pick a restaurant, gas station or shopping center in their city and write directions to it.
- Have each group write directions to a particular spot on your school's campus. Then have groups exchange directions and try to find each other's locations.

General

- Have those students who decided to build a shelter make an illustration of it.
- Ask students to collect information from the national park service about hiking preparation and safety. Then have them prepare an exhibit that shows what they have learned.
- Invite a member of a local search and rescue team to class to discuss recreational safety.
- Have students consult a national forest map of an area they find interesting and plan a hiking trip in that area.

Science

- Have students investigate and learn about first aid techniques.
- Have students research and report on edible and inedible plants.
- Have students research and report different ways to find or gather water.
- Have students research and report on various methods of determining location.

Copyright © 1998 Cottonwood Press, Inc. • 305 West Magnolia, Suite 398 • Fort Collins, Colorado 80521

For He's a Jolly Good Fellow
Describing a Famous Person

The problem to solve:

The famous Moose McGraw was in town yesterday, and you and your group got to meet him. Unfortunately, your friend Sylvia, who has been a big Moose fan ever since you have known her, was out of town and didn't get to see him. She's back home now and wants to know all about Moose. Describe your meeting so that she will feel she was there, too.

Copyright © 1998 Cottonwood Press, Inc. • 305 West Magnolia, Suite 398 • Fort Collins, Colorado 80521

Teacher Instructions

For He's a Jolly Good Fellow
Describing a Famous Person

"For He's a Jolly Good Fellow" asks students to describe a meeting with a famous person so well that a listener will feel almost as if he or she were there. Students must solve the problem of what to include in an effective description.

Getting started

- Organize the class into groups of three to five students each. Assign the roles of *leader, scribe, presenter* and *participant*. (See box on next page.)

- Go over the problem on page 37 with the class. You may reproduce the situation as a handout or overhead transparency, or you may present it orally to the class.

Creating questions

Supervise as the class brainstorms a list of questions. Ask, "What questions need to be answered to describe Moose McGraw?" Write the suggested questions on an overhead transparency or on the chalkboard. You may want to direct students to some of the support questions below.

Support questions:

- How old is Moose McGraw?
- Why is he well known?
- Why was he in your town?
- How tall is he? How much does he weigh?
- What are some special interests that he might have spoken about?
- Where does he live?

Answering the questions

In their small groups, have students decide which questions they think need to be answered in order to describe Moose McGraw. Set the minimum number of questions (five or more) at a level suited to the class. Also set a time limit for this portion of the activity. Thirty minutes is usually about right.

After the students decide on the questions, they should write answers to them. Remind students that while the answers are fictitious, they must be realistic and appropriate for the assignment.

Copyright © 1998 Cottonwood Press, Inc. • 305 West Magnolia, Suite 398 • Fort Collins, Colorado 80521

Teacher Instructions continued

Writing descriptions

Have students write their descriptions of Moose McGraw.

During the activity

While students are working on their answers to the questions, move from group to group, making sure that all students remain active during the work time. Review the specific responsibilities of each group member the first time you check in with a group. At other check-ins, encourage students to consider the following:

- Is everyone getting a chance to talk?
- How will this question help you describe Moose McGraw?
- Are you keeping track of the time? We have _____ minutes left.
- Do your questions work together to help you describe a person realistically?

Reporting

When the allotted time has passed, gather all the groups together again and have the presenters report to the class. The report from each group should include the questions selected, the answers given and the group's description of Moose McGraw. If desired, the rest of the class may ask questions, which any member of the reporting group may answer.

Assessing the activity

At the completion of the activity, use the "Closure Discussion" handout on page 14 to have students monitor their progress at working in small groups to solve problems.

Group Roles

Everyone in each group has an assigned role, and everyone has a responsibility to participate. The roles are:

- **Leader.** The leader is responsible for keeping the group on task, making sure all members participate and keeping track of time.

- **Scribe.** The scribe is responsible for writing down questions used and answers given, and for making any necessary charts or diagrams.

- **Presenter.** The presenter is responsible for explaining the group's activity during the reporting session.

- **Participant.** All participants have a responsibility to take part in the activity in a positive way.

Copyright © 1998 Cottonwood Press, Inc. • 305 West Magnolia, Suite 398 • Fort Collins, Colorado 80521

For He's a Jolly Good Fellow
Related Activities

Social studies

- Have students choose a famous person in history. Then ask them to write a set of interview questions and do research to find out what answers that person might have actually given to the questions.

English

- Have students write the script of a TV interview with Moose McGraw.
- Have students write a series of questions and use them to interview someone else in class. Then have them write a description about that person based on his or her answers.
- Have students write a thumbnail biography of Moose McGraw.
- Ask students to imagine being a guest at a community celebration for Moose McGraw. Have them write a speech for the mayor to give.
- Have students write the story of how Moose McGraw became so famous.
- Have students read a magazine or newspaper interview. Ask them to list all of the facts that they learned about the person being interviewed.

General

- Have students imagine that they have been chosen to give Moose McGraw a tour of your community. Have them make a list of places they would include on the tour.
- Have students watch an interview on television. Ask them to write down some of the interviewer's questions and the answers *they* would have given if they had been the person being interviewed.

Missing!
Describing a Missing Person

The problem to solve:

Chuck and Linda Johnson, your neighbors of more than two years, have told you they are not going away on vacation this year. But that was more than a week ago, and you haven't seen them since. They have not been answering their phone or their door bell. You decide to call the police.

What will you tell the detective? Be prepared to describe the Johnsons' appearance, their personalities and what they were wearing the last time you saw them. Since there are no available photographs of the Johnsons, and since they have no relatives in this part of the country, the police are depending on you and your group for information. Details are important.

Teacher Instructions

Missing!
Describing a Missing Person

"Missing!" requires students to solve the problem of creating adequate descriptions of two missing persons. The students must include details that will help police officers find and recognize the individuals.

Getting started

- Organize the class into groups of three to five students each. Assign the roles of *leader, scribe, presenter* and *participant*. (See box on next page.)
- Go over the problem on page 41 with the class. You may reproduce the situation as a handout or overhead transparency, or you may present it orally to the class.

Creating questions

Supervise as the class brainstorms a list of questions. Ask, "What questions need to be answered in order to describe and identify Chuck and Linda for the detective?" Write the suggested questions on an overhead transparency or on the chalkboard. You may want to direct students to some of the support questions below.

Support questions:

- How old are Chuck and Linda?
- What are their heights, weights and hair colors?
- Do they have any identifying features such as scars, birthmarks or tattoos?
- What details set them apart from other people on your block?
- What kind of car do they drive?
- Where do their families live?
- What are their hobbies?

Answering the questions

In their small groups, have students decide which questions they think need to be answered in order to give the detective a good description of Chuck and Linda. Set the minimum number of questions (five or more) at a level suited to the class. Also set a time limit for this portion of the activity. Thirty minutes is usually about right.

After the students decide on the questions, they should then write answers to them. Remind students that while the answers are fictitious, they must be realistic and appropriate for the assignment.

Copyright © 1998 Cottonwood Press, Inc. • 305 West Magnolia, Suite 398 • Fort Collins, Colorado 80521

Teacher Instructions continued

Writing the description

Have students write their descriptions.

During the activity

While students are working on their answers to the questions, move from group to group, making sure that all students remain active during the work time. Review the specific responsibilities of each group member the first time you check in with a group. At other check-ins, encourage students to consider the following:

- Is everyone getting a chance to talk?
- How will this question help identify the Johnsons?
- Are you keeping track of the time? We have _____ minutes left.
- What information are you including that may not be necessary?
- What are the most important points to be included in this description?

Reporting

When the allotted time has passed, gather all the groups together again and have the presenter report to the class. The report from each group should include the questions selected, the answers given and a brief description of the couple. If desired, the rest of the class may ask questions, which any member of the reporting group may answer.

Assessing the activity

At the completion of the activity, use the "Closure Discussion" handout on page 14 to have students monitor their progress at working in small groups to solve problems.

Group Roles

Everyone in each group has an assigned role, and everyone has a responsibility to participate. The roles are:

- **Leader.** The leader is responsible for keeping the group on task, making sure all members participate and keeping track of time.

- **Scribe.** The scribe is responsible for writing down questions used and answers given, and for making any necessary charts or diagrams.

- **Presenter.** The presenter is responsible for explaining the group's activity during the reporting session.

- **Participant.** All participants have a responsibility to take part in the activity in a positive way.

Copyright © 1998 Cottonwood Press, Inc. • 305 West Magnolia, Suite 398 • Fort Collins, Colorado 80521

Missing!
Related Activities

English

- Ask students to imagine that the case has been solved and the Johnsons have been found. Have them write the story of the search, including how the couple was found and what had happened to them.
- Have students write the script for a telephone conversation they might have with one of Chuck or Linda's relatives, explaining the problem.
- Have students research and report on a well-known case of a missing person.

General

- Invite a police officer to class to discuss techniques for reporting and finding missing persons.
- Have students list steps they might take to help in the search for Chuck and Linda, after they have spoken to the detective.
- Have students research and report on various organizations other than the police department that specialize in searching for missing persons.
- Invite a police artist to visit the class and demonstrate how he or she works.

Copyright © 1998 Cottonwood Press, Inc. • 305 West Magnolia, Suite 398 • Fort Collins, Colorado 80521

My Hero
Writing a Biographical Sketch

The problem to solve:

You are a writer who has set many of your stories and novels in Coasu, an imaginary country located deep in the Purple Mountains. Like our own country, Coasu has a national bird, a national flag and several national holidays. What Coasu *doesn't* have is any national heroes. That's because you haven't invented them yet!

Invent a hero for Coasu. What did he or she do that deserves respect? Write a brief summary of the hero's dramatic and inspiring life. With your biographical sketch, create a hero that the people of Coasu would be proud of — a person you might even want to write about in your next novel.

Teacher Instructions

My Hero
Writing a Biographical Sketch

With "My Hero," students solve a problem that might be encountered by a novelist. They create a fictional character — in this case, a national hero for the imaginary country of Coasu.

Getting started

- Organize the class into groups of three to five students each. Assign the roles of *leader, scribe, presenter* and *participant*. (See box on next page.)
- Go over the problem on page 45 with the class. You may reproduce the situation as a handout or overhead transparency, or you may present it orally to the class.

Creating questions

Supervise as the class brainstorms a list of questions. Ask, "What questions need to be answered in order to write the biography?" Write the suggested questions on an overhead transparency or on the chalkboard. You may want to direct students to some of the support questions below.

Support questions:

- Is the hero a man or a woman?
- What is his or her name?
- How long ago did this person live?
- Where did this person live?
- What did this person accomplish?
- What makes this person a hero?
- What was the greatest moment in this person's life?

Answering the questions

In their small groups, have students decide which questions they think need to be answered in order to write a biographical sketch of a hero's life. Set the minimum number of questions (five or more) at a level suited to the class. Also set a time limit for this portion of the activity. Thirty to forty-five minutes is usually about right.

After students decide on the questions, they should write answers to them. Remind students that while the answers are fictitious, they must be realistic and appropriate for the assignment.

Copyright © 1998 Cottonwood Press, Inc. • 305 West Magnolia, Suite 398 • Fort Collins, Colorado 80521

Teacher Instructions continued

Writing sketches

Have students write their biographical sketches.

During the activity

While students are working on their answers to the questions, move from group to group, making sure that all students remain active during the work time. Review the specific responsibilities of each group member the first time you check in with a group. At other check-ins, encourage students to consider the following:

- Is everyone getting a chance to talk?
- Whom have you chosen to write about?
- How will this question help you tell about your historical figure?
- Are you keeping track of the time? We have _____ minutes left.
- Are you telling the events of this person's life sequentially?
- Have you created events that would make current citizens of Coasu admire your historical figure?

Reporting

When the allotted time has passed, gather all the groups together again and have the presenters report to the class. The report from each group should include the questions selected, the answers given and the biographical sketch. If desired, the rest of the class may ask questions which any member of the reporting group may answer.

Assessing the activity

At the completion of the activity, use the "Closure Discussion" handout on page 14 to have students monitor their progress at working in small groups to solve problems.

Group Roles

Everyone in each group has an assigned role, and everyone has a responsibility to participate. The roles are:

- **Leader.** The leader is responsible for keeping the group on task, making sure all members participate and keeping track of time.
- **Scribe.** The scribe is responsible for writing down questions used and answers given, and for making any necessary charts or diagrams.
- **Presenter.** The presenter is responsible for explaining the group's activity during the reporting session.
- **Participant.** All participants have a responsibility to take part in the activity in a positive way.

Copyright © 1998 Cottonwood Press, Inc. • 305 West Magnolia, Suite 398 • Fort Collins, Colorado 80521

My Hero
Writing a Biographical Sketch

English

- Have students write a paragraph showing how their hero is like and unlike another hero of their choice.
- Ask the class to brainstorm a list of some heroes of their generation. Have them elaborate on the qualities that make these people heroic.

Social studies

- Have students research and report on a national hero of another country.
- Have students research and report on monuments that have been built to honor heroes in American history.
- Have students make a map of the country of Coasu, including historic sites related to the deeds of their hero.

Art

- Have students draw a portrait of the new hero of Coasu.
- Have students design a postage stamp to honor the hero from Coasu.
- Have students make a model of a monument to be built in honor of their hero.
- Ask students which of their hero's qualities stands out the most. Have them create a slogan and design a sampler or a plaque that would display this characteristic.

Copyright © 1998 Cottonwood Press, Inc. • 305 West Magnolia, Suite 398 • Fort Collins, Colorado 80521

Welcome Mat
Getting to Know a Community

The problem to solve:

Maluc and Farisa, two students your age, have come a great distance to stay with a family in your area for a week. Although they speak English, Maluc and Farisa are not at all familiar with your town or city. Since you know the community well, you have been asked to show them around and to help them in any way possible.

Prepare an activity schedule that will help Maluc and Farisa learn as much as possible about your community and the people who live there.

Copyright © 1998 Cottonwood Press, Inc. • 305 West Magnolia, Suite 398 • Fort Collins, Colorado 80521

Teacher Instructions

Welcome Mat
Getting to Know a Community

With "Welcome Mat," students decide what to include on an activity schedule for two foreign students visiting your community for a week. They solve the problem of how to give visitors an understanding of a community in a short time.

Getting started

- Organize the class into groups of three to five students each. Assign the roles of *leader, scribe, presenter* and *participant*. (See box on next page.)
- Go over the problem on page 49 with the class. You may reproduce the situation as a handout or overhead transparency, or you may present it orally to the class.

Creating questions

Supervise as the class brainstorms a list of questions. Ask, "What questions need to be answered to create an activity schedule for Maluc and Farisa?" Write the suggested questions on an overhead transparency or on the chalkboard. You may want to direct students to some of the support questions below.

Support questions:

- What is unique about our community?
- What special interests do Maluc and Farisa have?
- What kind of transportation will we use?
- Are there any local celebrities we would like them to meet?
- What special community celebrations will take place while they are visiting?

Answering the questions

In their small groups, have students decide which questions they think need to be answered in order to prepare an activity schedule. Set the minimum number of questions (five or more) at a level suited to the class. Also set a time limit for this portion of the activity. Thirty minutes is usually about right.

After students decide on the questions, they should then write answers to them. Remind students that while the answers are fictitious, they must be realistic and appropriate for the assignment.

Making lists

Have students make their list of activities.

Teacher Instructions continued

During the activity

While students are working on their answers to the questions, move from group to group, making sure that all students remain active during the work time. Review the specific responsibilities of each group member the first time you check in with a group. At other check-ins, encourage students to consider the following:

- Is everyone getting a chance to talk?
- How will this question help with planning the activity schedule?
- Are you keeping track of the time? We have _____ minutes left.
- What is the order in which you will do these things with Maluc and Farisa?
- Will you be walking, driving or riding a bus? How will you get from one place to another?

Reporting

When the allotted time has passed, gather all the groups together again, and have the presenters report to the class. The report from each group should include the questions selected, the answers given and the activity schedule. If desired, the rest of the class may ask questions, which any member of the reporting group may answer.

Assessing the activity

At the completion of the activity, use the "Closure Discussion" handout on page 14 to have students monitor their progress at working in small groups to solve problems.

Group Roles

Everyone in each group has an assigned role, and everyone has a responsibility to participate. The roles are:

- **Leader.** The leader is responsible for keeping the group on task, making sure all members participate and keeping track of time.

- **Scribe.** The scribe is responsible for writing down questions used and answers given, and for making any necessary charts or diagrams.

- **Presenter.** The presenter is responsible for explaining the group's activity during the reporting session.

- **Participant.** All participants have a responsibility to take part in the activity in a positive way.

Copyright © 1998 Cottonwood Press, Inc. • 305 West Magnolia, Suite 398 • Fort Collins, Colorado 80521

Welcome Mat
Related Activities

English

- Have students design and write a brochure or guide book filled with information about their community.
- Have students write a letter to Maluc and Farisa, introducing themselves and describing what they are likely to expect from people their age in the community.

Social studies

- Have students research a city in another country and list tourist attractions they would like to visit.
- Using the suggestions generated by all of the groups, take a field trip around your community.

Art

- Have students make post cards that Maluc and Farisa would send home. The front of the card should have a picture. A short message should be written on the back.
- Have students make a poster advertising an attraction in their community.

Teacher Instructions

Games People Play
Inventing Games

The problem to solve:

The Thrill-A-Minute Game Company is in a state of crisis. For many years, it has been making popular board games like "Billionaire" and "Avalanche," but now it has run out of ideas. None of the game designers can come up with a new game that will excite young people.

The company is turning to you to invent a new game specifically for young people. Make up the rules for the game, and design the board and pieces. If you have enough time, construct the game and play it with members of your group.

Teacher Instructions

Games People Play
Inventing Games

"Games People Play" requires students to solve a problem that might be encountered by a manufacturer of board games. The students must design a game that will appeal specifically to young people.

Getting started

- Gather materials for making games. Some suggestions: construction paper, poster board, file cards, cardboard, pens, pencils, crayons, markers, rulers, glue, glitter, paint, dice and spinners. You may also want to have classic board games on hand as models for this activity.

- Organize the class into groups of three to five students each. Assign the roles of *leader, scribe, presenter* and *participant*. (See box on next page.)

- Go over the problem on page 53 with the class. You may reproduce the situation as a handout or overhead transparency, or you may present it orally to the class.

Creating questions

Supervise as the class brainstorms a list of questions. Ask, "What questions need to be answered in order to create a new board game?" Write the suggested questions on an overhead transparency or on the chalkboard. You may want to direct students to some of the support questions below.

Support questions:

- What age group of young people will we be targeting?
- How many people can play the game?
- How long does it take to play?
- How do the pieces move?
- What is the object of the game?

Answering the questions

In their small groups, have students decide which questions they think need to be answered in order to create the new game. Set the minimum number of questions (five or more) at a level suited to the class. Also set a time limit for this portion of the activity. Forty-five to sixty minutes may be necessary.

After students decide on the questions, they should write answers to them. Remind students that while the answers are fictitious, they must be realistic and appropriate for the assignment.

Copyright © 1998 Cottonwood Press, Inc. • 305 West Magnolia, Suite 398 • Fort Collins, Colorado 80521

Teacher Instructions continued

Creating the game

Have students create their games.

During the activity

While students are working on their answers to the questions, move from group to group, making sure that all students remain active during the work time. Review the specific responsibilities of each group member the first time you check in with a group. At other check-ins, encourage students to consider the following:

- Is everyone getting a chance to talk?
- How will this question help you create a game?
- Are you keeping track of the time? We have _____ minutes left.
- What is the object of the game?
- How long do you think it will take to play this game?

Reporting

When the allotted time has passed, gather all the groups together again and have the presenters report to the class. The report from each group should include the questions selected and the answers given. The presenter should then display the game they created and explain briefly how it is played. If desired, the rest of the class may ask questions, which any member of the reporting group may answer.

Assessing the activity

At the completion of the activity, use the "Closure Discussion" handout on page 14 to have students monitor their progress at working in small groups to solve problems.

Group Roles

Everyone in each group has an assigned role, and everyone has a responsibility to participate. The roles are:

- **Leader.** The leader is responsible for keeping the group on task, making sure all members participate and keeping track of time.

- **Scribe.** The scribe is responsible for writing down questions used and answers given, and for making any necessary charts or diagrams.

- **Presenter.** The presenter is responsible for explaining the group's activity during the reporting session.

- **Participant.** All participants have a responsibility to take part in the activity in a positive way.

Copyright © 1998 Cottonwood Press, Inc. • 305 West Magnolia, Suite 398 • Fort Collins, Colorado 80521

Games People Play
Related Activities

Social studies

- Have students research and report on games played in other countries.
- Have students research and report on the history of a classic game like checkers or backgammon.
- Have students interview a grandparent about games played during his or her childhood.

General

- Organize all of the games that the students make into an activity center. Encourage students to try out the games during free time.
- Have students make games to be used with children in a younger grade level, and donate the finished games to an appropriate class.
- Have students design other games based on specific topics — math facts, geometry concepts, vocabulary definitions, science or social studies information, for example.
- Ask students to convert their game into a television game show. Have them videotape one of the mock game shows.

Art

- Have students design a container for their new game.
- Have students write a television commercial for their game and then draw a story board for the commercial.

Math

- Have students study the odds of winning tic-tac-toe or other games of chance.

Myth Maker
Mythology

The problem to solve:

Peraclautus — wise man, writer, entertainer and teller of myths in a faraway land — has run out of tales. After so many stories about Zeus and Hera, Apollo and Artemis, he simply cannot think of anything more to add. That wouldn't be so bad, except for the fact that Peraclautus is under contract to produce four new myths a year — one for each season.

Because he has heard that all of you know a great deal about myths and how they are made, Peraclautus urgently requests that you help him out by inventing a new myth. You may use traditional Greek characters or make up your own. Remember that mythical gods and goddesses have many human characteristics. The mythical stories contain messages and morals that teach us about nature and human life.

Teacher Instructions

Myth Maker
Mythology

With "Myth Maker," students create a new myth involving traditional Greek gods and goddesses or new characters. In doing so, they must address the problems of deciding what characters to include, what messages or morals to teach and how to do so in an entertaining way.

Getting started

- Read some Greek myths to the class and/or have students read some myths on their own.
- With students, review an age-appropriate list of Greek gods and goddesses and their traits.
- Organize the class into groups of three to five students each. Assign the roles of *leader, scribe, presenter* and *participant*. (See box on next page.)
- Go over the problem on page 57 with the class. You may reproduce the situation as a handout or overhead transparency, or you may present it orally to the class.

Creating questions

Supervise as the class brainstorms a list of questions. Ask, "What questions need to be answered in order to invent a new myth?" Write the suggested questions on an overhead transparency or on the chalkboard. You may want to direct students to some of the support questions below.

Support questions:

- Who will be the main characters of the myth?
- Where will the myth take place?
- What are some events that will happen in the story?
- What is the message or moral of the story?

Answering the questions

In their small groups, have students decide which questions they think need to be answered in order to invent the new myth. Set the minimum number of questions (five or more) at a level suited to the class. Also set a time limit for this portion of the activity. Thirty to forty-five minutes is usually about right.

After students decide on the questions, they should write answers to them. Remind students that while the answers are fictitious, they must be realistic and appropriate for myths.

Copyright © 1998 Cottonwood Press, Inc. • 305 West Magnolia, Suite 398 • Fort Collins, Colorado 80521

Teacher Instructions continued

Creating myths

Students should use their answers to help them write their own myths.

During the activity

While students are working on their answers to the questions, move from group to group, making sure that all students remain active during the work time. Review the specific responsibilities of each group member the first time you check in with a group. At other check-ins, encourage students to consider the following:

- Is everyone getting a chance to talk?
- How will this question help with the story line of your myth?
- Are you keeping track of the time? We have _____ minutes left.
- How does your myth apply to human life?
- Do your gods and goddesses have some human characteristics?

Reporting

When the allotted time has passed, gather all the groups together again and have the presenters report to the class. The report from each group should include the questions selected, the answers given and the myth created. The myth can be told by the presenter alone or with the help of the rest of the group. If desired, the rest of the class may ask questions, which any member of the reporting group may answer.

Assessing the activity

At the completion of the activity, use the "Closure Discussion" handout on page 14 to have students monitor their progress at working in small groups to solve problems.

Group Roles

Everyone in each group has an assigned role, and everyone has a responsibility to participate. The roles are:

- **Leader.** The leader is responsible for keeping the group on task, making sure all members participate and keeping track of time.

- **Scribe.** The scribe is responsible for writing down questions used and answers given, and for making any necessary charts or diagrams.

- **Presenter.** The presenter is responsible for explaining the group's activity during the reporting session.

- **Participant.** All participants have a responsibility to take part in the activity in a positive way.

Copyright © 1998 Cottonwood Press, Inc. • 305 West Magnolia, Suite 398 • Fort Collins, Colorado 80521

Myth Maker
Related Activities

English

- Have the class as a whole collect local legends and myths. Record them in a notebook.
- Have students read myths from another culture (Norse or Native American myths, for example) and compare them with Greek myths.
- Have students write a play using the plot for the myth developed by their group.
- Ask students to select a god or goddess with a quality or characteristic they admire. Have them each write a new story involving that figure.
- Many myths were created in order to explain mysterious phenomena in the world. Ask students to think of an occurrence they don't understand and create a myth to explain it. They may want to explain thunder, lightning or sunsets, for example.
- Ask students to think of a superstition. Have them write a short myth about how and why that superstition came about. They might write about why walking under a ladder is bad luck, or why four-leaf clovers are good luck, for example.
- Have students write a character description of a god or goddess from their myth.

Social studies

- Have students research and report on archaeological digs in Greece.

Art

- Have students draw the characters in their myth, or a scene from the myth.

It's the Law
Making Rules

The problem to solve:

It is the year 2200. You have been chosen to travel aboard the spaceship "Greatness," which is headed toward deepest space. One million miles (three days) into the trip, you learn that the basic procedure manual is missing. That means that there are no written rules or laws to govern behavior on the spaceship.

It is up to your group to make up rules that you can live by during the long voyage. How will things be run? Who will lead? What will be the penalty for breaking the rules? You will have to answer these and many other questions if your trip is to go smoothly and you are to return safely to earth.

Copyright © 1998 Cottonwood Press, Inc. • 305 West Magnolia, Suite 398 • Fort Collins, Colorado 80521

Teacher Instructions

It's the Law
Making Rules

With "It's the Law," students must come up with a plan for governing a group of travelers on a spaceship. They must solve the problem of deciding upon a workable set of rules for a group to follow.

Getting started

- Organize the class into groups of three to five students each. Assign the roles of *leader, scribe, presenter* and *participant*. (See box on next page.)
- Go over the problem on page 61 with the class. You may reproduce the situation as a handout or overhead transparency, or you may present it orally to the class.

Creating questions

Supervise as the class brainstorms a list of questions. Ask, "What questions need to be answered in order to form a list of rules for spaceship travelers?" Write the suggested questions on an overhead transparency or on the chalkboard. You may want to direct students to some of the support questions below.

Support questions:

- What is the purpose of the trip?
- How will we select a leader?
- How will we agree on what the rules should be?
- How will rules be enforced and by whom?
- What will be considered illegal acts?
- What are the responsibilities of the travelers under these rules?
- What are the consequences for breaking the rules?

Answering the questions

In their small groups, have students decide which questions they think need to be answered in order to write a list of rules for the space travelers. Set the minimum number of questions (five or more) at a level suited to the class. Also set a time limit for this portion of the activity. Thirty minutes is usually about right.

After the students decide on the questions, they should write answers to them. Remind students that while the answers are fictitious, they must be realistic and appropriate for the assignment.

Teacher Instructions continued

Writing the rules

Have students write the list of rules.

During the activity

While students are working on their answers to the questions, move from group to group, making sure that all students remain active during the work time. Review the specific responsibilities of each group member the first time you check in with a group. At other check-ins, encourage students to consider the following:

- Is everyone getting a chance to talk?
- How will this question help with the decisions about rules?
- Are you keeping track of the time? We have _____ minutes left.
- Is it better to have a lot of rules or just a few rules? Why or why not?
- Why is a particular rule necessary?
- How will you enforce this rule?
- Does everyone in your group agree that this rule should be included?

Reporting

When the allotted time has passed, gather all the groups together again and have the presenters report to the class. The report from each group should include the questions the group selected, the answers given and the list of rules. If desired, the rest of the class may ask questions, which any member of the reporting group may answer.

Assessing the activity

At the completion of the activity, use the "Closure Discussion" handout on page 14 to have students monitor their progress at working in small groups to solve problems.

Group Roles

Everyone in each group has an assigned role, and everyone has a responsibility to participate. The roles are:

- **Leader.** The leader is responsible for keeping the group on task, making sure all members participate and keeping track of time.

- **Scribe.** The scribe is responsible for writing down questions used and answers given, and for making any necessary charts or diagrams.

- **Presenter.** The presenter is responsible for explaining the group's activity during the reporting session.

- **Participant.** All participants have a responsibility to take part in the activity in a positive way.

Copyright © 1998 Cottonwood Press, Inc. • 305 West Magnolia, Suite 398 • Fort Collins, Colorado 80521

It's the Law
Related Activities

Social studies

- Have students research and report on the structure of the U.S. Constitution.
- Invite a local city council member, county commissioner or state legislator to come to class to discuss the procedures for making laws.
- Take a field trip to a decision-making body (state legislature, city council, school board, etc.) in session.
- Lead a class discussion about when and why people have to have rules. Have students review the rules of your school and try to determine why each was made.
- Have students devise a process for making classroom rules and then create a classroom constitution using their process.

Science

- Have students plan the voyage of the "Greatness," using astronomical books and maps.

General

- Have students draw diagrams of the "Greatness," including a floor plan, a cross section view and an exterior view.
- Obtain handbooks from other schools. Have students compare the rules with the rules of your school.

Math

- Have students figure out how fast they would have to be travelling in order to go one million miles in three days.

Time Marches On
Filling a Time Capsule

The problem to solve:

Have you heard? Local historians are filling a time capsule with objects and documents from the area where you live. The materials will be placed in an earthquake-proof container. On its surface, instructions for opening the container will be written in ten languages and also in pictures. If all goes well, the time capsule will remain untouched until the year 2200.

Since all of you know the area so well, you have been asked to help select what should go inside the capsule. You may put inside as many things as you like, but each article should clearly show something about what it is like to live here and now. Each article should show what people of this day and age find important.

Your choices should be so clear that beings from the future (even alien beings!) can learn a great deal about the people who live today in your area of the country.

Copyright © 1998 Cottonwood Press, Inc. • 305 West Magnolia, Suite 398 • Fort Collins, Colorado 80521

Teacher Instructions

Time Marches On
Filling a Time Capsule

With "Time Marches On," students solve a problem that might be encountered by a local historian preparing information for a time capsule. They must decide what items to include in a time capsule representing life in their community in the late 20th century.

Getting started

- Organize the class into groups of three to five students each. Assign the roles of *leader, scribe, presenter* and *participant*. (See box on next page.)
- Go over the problem on page 65 with the class. You may reproduce the situation as a handout or overhead transparency, or you may present it orally to the class.

Creating questions

Supervise as the class brainstorms a list of questions. Ask, "What questions need to be answered in order to decide what to include in the time capsule?" Write the suggested questions on an overhead transparency or on the chalkboard. You may want to direct students to some of the support questions below.

Support questions:

- What do we want future people to know about us?
- What are some characteristics of our lifestyle that we can show?
- How many items about any single characteristic will we include?
- What possibilities for information do we have — visual, audio, printed, etc.?
- What limitations do we have about what can be included?

Answering the questions

In their small groups, have students decide which questions they think need to be answered in order to decide what should be included in the time capsule. Set the minimum number of questions (five or more) at a level suited to the class. Also set a time limit for this portion of the activity. Thirty minutes is usually about right.

After the students decide on the questions, they should write answers to them. Remind students that while the answers are fictitious, they must be realistic and appropriate for the assignment.

Making lists

Have students prepare their list of selections for the time capsule.

Copyright © 1998 Cottonwood Press, Inc. • 305 West Magnolia, Suite 398 • Fort Collins, Colorado 80521

Teacher Instructions continued

During the activity

While students are working on their answers to the questions, move from group to group, making sure that all students remain active during the work time. Review the specific responsibilities of each group member the first time you check in with a group. At other check-ins, encourage students to consider the following:

- Is everyone getting a chance to talk?
- How will this question help with the decisions about what can be included?
- Are you keeping track of the time? We have ____ minutes left.
- What decisions can you make from your answers to the questions?
- What does the item you have chosen for the time capsule show about our current lifestyle?

Reporting

When the allotted time has passed, gather all the groups together again and have the presenters report to the class. The report from each group should include the questions selected, the answers given and the list of items to be included in the time capsule. If desired, the rest of the class may ask questions, which any member of the reporting group may answer.

Assessing the activity

At the completion of the activity, use the "Closure Discussion" handout on page 14 to have students monitor their progress at working in small groups to solve problems.

Group Roles

Everyone in each group has an assigned role, and everyone has a responsibility to participate. The roles are:

- **Leader.** The leader is responsible for keeping the group on task, making sure all members participate and keeping track of time.

- **Scribe.** The scribe is responsible for writing down questions used and answers given, and for making any necessary charts or diagrams.

- **Presenter.** The presenter is responsible for explaining the group's activity during the reporting session.

- **Participant.** All participants have a responsibility to take part in the activity in a positive way.

Copyright © 1998 Cottonwood Press, Inc. • 305 West Magnolia, Suite 398 • Fort Collins, Colorado 80521

Time Marches On
Related Activities

Social studies

- Have students consider an ancient civilization they have studied. Ask them to make a list of artifacts that the people of that civilization could have included in a time capsule.
- Have students consider modern life in a foreign country they have studied. Ask them to list items appropriate for a time capsule from that country.
- Have students make a historical time line of your community to include in a time capsule.

English

- Have students write a letter to someone from the future, perhaps a future relative. In the letter, they should describe their life today.

Science

- Have students research the geology of your area. Where should the time capsule be buried to ensure that it will be safe from storms, erosion, floods and other natural disasters?

General

- Have each student make his or her own personal time capsule. Remind students to include in their capsules things which convey their unique personalities.
- Have students write a list of questions a person from the year 2200 might ask about life today.
- Have students create a time capsule to be opened by students next year. Ask them to include tips for functioning in your class. Also, have them create a map that will guide next year's students to the capsule.
- Have students choose a location for the capsule and list the reasons the site is a good choice.

Art

- Have students design the outside of their time capsule, trying to make it appealing to unknown beings of the future.

Student Instructions

Play Ball!
Finding Uses for Extra Things

The problem to solve:

Because of an ordering mistake, one million baseballs will be delivered to this school next week. The manufacturer of these balls is going out of business and cannot possibly take them back. The school athletic department can use only about a hundred of the baseballs, and there really is no room to store the rest of them.

That is where you come in. Make a long list of suggestions for what could be done with so many baseballs. (No, you cannot just throw them away. That would be wasteful.)

Copyright © 1998 Cottonwood Press, Inc. • 305 West Magnolia, Suite 398 • Fort Collins, Colorado 80521

Teacher Instructions

Play Ball!
Finding Uses for Extra Things

"Play Ball!" requires students to find uses for an over-supply of a product. They must come up with a solution for the problem of what to do with one million baseballs.

Getting started

- Organize the class into groups of three to five students each. Assign the roles of *leader, scribe, presenter* and *participant*. (See box on next page.)

- Go over the problem on page 69 with the class. You may reproduce the situation as a handout or overhead transparency, or you may present it orally to the class.

Creating questions

Supervise as the class brainstorms a list of questions. Ask, "What questions need to be answered in order to find a use for a million baseballs?" Write the suggested questions on an overhead transparency or on the chalkboard. You may want to direct students to some of the support questions below.

Support questions:
- Who uses baseballs?
- How often do baseballs need to be replaced?
- What are some other uses for baseballs?
- What are some methods we can use to ship the baseballs to other locations?
- What else can be constructed with the materials from which baseballs are made?

Answering the questions

In their small groups, have students decide which questions they think need to be answered in order to find uses for the baseballs. Set the minimum number of questions (five or more) at a level suited to the class. Also set a time limit for this portion of the activity. Thirty minutes is usually about right.

After students decide on the questions, they should write answers to them. Remind the students that while the answers are fictitious, they must be realistic and appropriate for the assignment.

Making lists

Have students prepare their lists.

Copyright © 1998 Cottonwood Press, Inc. • 305 West Magnolia, Suite 398 • Fort Collins, Colorado 80521

Teacher Instructions continued

During the activity

While students are working on their answers to the questions, move from group to group, making sure that all students remain active during the work time. Review the specific responsibilities of each group member the first time you check in with a group. At other check-ins, encourage students to consider the following:

- Is everyone getting a chance to talk?
- How will this question help solve the problem of an enormous surplus of baseballs?
- Are you keeping track of the time? We have _____ minutes left.
- How will you organize distribution of the baseballs?
- Who will take responsibility for the baseballs when they arrive?
- Are your uses realistic?

Reporting

When the allotted time has passed, gather all the groups together again and have the presenters report to the class. The report from each group should include the questions selected, the answers given and the list of alternative uses for baseballs. If desired, the rest of the class may ask questions, which any member of the reporting group may answer.

Assessing the activity

At the completion of the activity, use the "Closure Discussion" handout on page 14 to have students monitor their progress at working in small groups to solve problems.

Group Roles

Everyone in each group has an assigned role, and everyone has a responsibility to participate. The roles are:

- **Leader.** The leader is responsible for keeping the group on task, making sure all members participate and keeping track of time.

- **Scribe.** The scribe is responsible for writing down questions used and answers given, and for making any necessary charts or diagrams.

- **Presenter.** The presenter is responsible for explaining the group's activity during the reporting session.

- **Participant.** All participants have a responsibility to take part in the activity in a positive way.

Copyright © 1998 Cottonwood Press, Inc. • 305 West Magnolia, Suite 398 • Fort Collins, Colorado 80521

Play Ball!
Related Activities

English

- Have students research and report on the development of the game of baseball.
- Have students create a dictionary of definitions for baseball jargon.
- Have students write an essay agreeing or disagreeing with this statement: Baseball is the great American pastime.
- Have students compare and contrast their favorite baseball movies.

General

- Invite a local spokesperson for an environmental group to discuss ways in which your community reuses materials.
- Have students design and make a model of a gadget or toy which has a baseball as one of its components.
- Have students make a chart showing as many different kinds of sports balls as possible. The chart should include a picture of each type of ball, as well as an explanation of its use.
- Have students interview at least five adults for their ideas of how to use the over-supply of baseballs.
- Ask students to invent a new game that uses at least one baseball. Ask them to write a description of their game, including basic rules.

Math

- With the class, create a display that shows how many 1,000,000 is.
- Have students determine approximately how much space 1,000,000 baseballs would take up.

Social studies

- Have students research and report on popular ball games from other countries (cricket in England, for example).

Copyright © 1998 Cottonwood Press, Inc. • 305 West Magnolia, Suite 398 • Fort Collins, Colorado 80521

Something Special
Choosing Products for a Catalog

The problem to solve:

SchoolLife is a new company that intends to produce a catalog filled with "perfect gifts for kids." Knowing that young people, in general, have far less money to spend than adults, the company plans to send the catalog only to parents and grandparents.

The problem is that SchoolLife knows nothing about the tastes and preferences of young people today. To get a handle on products and services that interest kids, the company is asking you, experts on the tastes and opinions of young people, to make up a list of original and unforgettable items to be included in the catalog.

SchoolLife wants to offer a mix of both expensive and inexpensive items and services. It also must take into consideration the feelings and attitudes of the adults buying the items. It is important that the catalog be filled with unforgettable gifts that appeal to young people, but they must also be items that adults will be willing to buy.

Teacher Instructions

Something Special
Choosing Products for a Catalog

With "Something Special," students solve a problem that might be encountered by a direct mail company. They create a list of products for a catalog aimed at parents and grandparents who are buying gifts for the young people in their lives.

Getting started

- Organize the class into groups of three to five students each. Assign the roles of *leader, scribe, presenter* and *participant*. (See box on next page.)

- Go over the problem on page 73 with the class. You may reproduce the situation as a handout or overhead transparency, or you may present it orally to the class.

Creating questions

Supervise as the class brainstorms a list of questions. Ask, "What questions need to be answered in order to make a list of items for the catalog?" Write the suggested questions on an overhead transparency or on the chalkboard. You may want to direct students to some of the support questions below.

Support questions:
- How old are the kids being targeted by this catalog?
- What are some special interests of kids of this age?
- What kinds of gifts do adults like to give?
- About how many items will be on the list?
- What different categories of gifts should be included?
- Are there any intangible gifts which could be included in the catalog — gifts such as activities or trips, rather than *things*?

Answering the questions

In their small groups, have students decide which questions they think need to be answered in order to make a list of items for the catalog. Set the minimum number of questions (five or more) at a level suited to the class. Also set a time limit for this portion of the activity. Thirty minutes is usually about right.

After students decide on the questions, they should write answers to them. Remind students that while the answers are fictitious, they must be realistic and appropriate for the assignment.

Copyright © 1998 Cottonwood Press, Inc. • 305 West Magnolia, Suite 398 • Fort Collins, Colorado 80521

Teacher Instructions continued

Writing lists

Have students write their list of items for the catalog.

During the activity

While students are working on their answers to the questions, move from group to group, making sure that all students remain active during the work time. Review the specific responsibilities of each group member the first time you check in with a group. At other check-ins, encourage students to consider the following:

- Is everyone getting a chance to talk?
- How will this question help with choosing items for the list?
- Are you keeping track of the time? We have _____ minutes left.
- How many items of one kind do you have?
- What items might be sold to go with this one?
- Who would find this item appealing?
- Would adults approve of having this item in the catalog?

Reporting

When the allotted time has passed, gather all the groups together again and have the presenters report to the class. The report from each group should include the questions selected, the answers given and the list of items. If desired, the rest of the class may ask questions which any member of the reporting group may answer.

Assessing the activity

At the completion of the activity, use the "Closure Discussion" handout on page 14 to have students monitor their progress at working in small groups to solve problems.

Group Roles

Everyone in each group has an assigned role, and everyone has a responsibility to participate. The roles are:

- **Leader.** The leader is responsible for keeping the group on task, making sure all members participate and keeping track of time.

- **Scribe.** The scribe is responsible for writing down questions used and answers given, and for making any necessary charts or diagrams.

- **Presenter.** The presenter is responsible for explaining the group's activity during the reporting session.

- **Participant.** All participants have a responsibility to take part in the activity in a positive way.

Copyright © 1998 Cottonwood Press, Inc. • 305 West Magnolia, Suite 398 • Fort Collins, Colorado 80521

Something Special
Related Activities

English

- Have students write an advertising letter introducing SchoolLife's new catalog to the adults who will receive it.
- Have students research and report on the founders of well-known catalog companies like Sears and J.C. Penney.
- Have students write a sales description of a few of their favorite items. (They may also want to include the price and a drawing of the item.)

Math

- Give students an imaginary budget of $300 and a set of catalogs. Have them select exactly five gifts for themselves, without exceeding their budget. Remind them to include tax and shipping and handling charges in their figures.

Art

- Have students draw a cover for SchoolLife's new catalog.

The Play Is the Thing
Writing a Skit

The problem to solve:

Welcome to the Playwright's Club. Every week, the members of this organization meet to write new plays and skits to perform. This week, you and your group have been invited to join them.

First your group must invent a character for each person in the group to play. Describe each character in detail. The characters may be young, old, honest, funny, good-hearted, evil-minded — whatever you decide.

After you have the characters, create a plot or story that includes them. Be sure your plot includes a problem and a solution. Be sure also that it is realistic to solve the problem in a short 10–15 minute play.

Next, write dialogue. Make the characters talk to one another, saying things that follow the plot of your story.

Finally, perform your skit for the rest of the class.

Teacher Instructions

The Play Is the Thing
Writing a Skit

With "The Play Is the Thing" students write a skit and perform it for the rest of the class. They must solve the problem of making characters, plot and dialogue work together.

Getting started

- Before the lesson, have students read short plays or skits.
- Organize the class into groups of three to five students each. Assign the roles of *leader, scribe, presenter* and *participant*. (See box on next page.)
- Go over the problem on page 77 with the class. You may reproduce the situation as a handout or overhead transparency, or you may present it orally to the class.

Creating questions

Supervise as the class brainstorms a list of questions. Ask, "What questions need to be answered in order to write and perform the skit?" Write the suggested questions on an overhead transparency or on the chalkboard. You may want to direct students to some of the support questions below.

Support questions:
- Who are the characters?
- During what time period does the story take place?
- How are we introduced to the characters?
- What is the setting?
- Is the plot realistic for a 10–15 minute play?

Answering the questions

In their small groups, have students decide which questions they think need to be answered in order to write and perform their skit. Set the minimum number of questions (five or more) at a level suited to the class. Also set a time limit for this portion of the activity. Forty-five to sixty minutes or more may be necessary.

After students decide on the questions, they should answer them. Remind students that while the answers are fictitious, they must be realistic and appropriate for the assignment.

Writing scripts

Have students write their scripts. With younger students, it may be necessary to provide lists of characters and plot ideas to choose from.

Copyright © 1998 Cottonwood Press, Inc. • 305 West Magnolia, Suite 398 • Fort Collins, Colorado 80521

Teacher Instructions continued

During the activity

While students are working on their answers to the questions, move from group to group, making sure that all students remain active during the work time. Review the specific responsibilities of each group member the first time you check in with a group. At other check-ins, encourage students to consider the following:

- Is everyone getting a chance to talk?
- Who are your characters?
- How will this question help you define the plot?
- Are you keeping track of the time? We have _____ minutes left.
- Have you practiced reading the different roles of this skit?

Reporting

When the allotted time has passed, gather all the groups together again and have the presenter from each group report to the class. The report from each group should include the questions selected, the answers given and the list of characters. If desired, the rest of the class may ask questions which any member of the reporting group may answer. The group should then present the skit, with each member taking a role.

Assessing the activity

At the completion of the activity, use the "Closure Discussion" handout on page 14 to have students monitor their progress at working in small groups to solve problems.

Group Roles

Everyone in each group has an assigned role, and everyone has a responsibility to participate. The roles are:

- **Leader.** The leader is responsible for keeping the group on task, making sure all members participate and keeping track of time.

- **Scribe.** The scribe is responsible for writing down questions used and answers given, and for making any necessary charts or diagrams.

- **Presenter.** The presenter is responsible for explaining the group's activity during the reporting session.

- **Participant.** All participants have a responsibility to take part in the activity in a positive way.

Copyright © 1998 Cottonwood Press, Inc. • 305 West Magnolia, Suite 398 • Fort Collins, Colorado 80521

The Play Is the Thing
Related Activities

English

- Ask students to write a short story using the plot and characters of their group's skit.
- Have students read several drama reviews in the newspaper. Ask them to imagine they are drama critics and write a column reviewing one of the skits performed in class.
- Have students write a short paragraph about each actor in their group, to include in a program for their play.

General

- Have the class read a well-known play together.
- Take a field trip to a local theater for the performance of a play.

Art

- Have students design a costume for one or more of the characters in their skit.
- Have students create programs and/or posters advertising their plays.
- Ask students to make puppets and perform their group's skit as a puppet show.

A Place of Our Own
Planning a Community

The problem to solve:

The government has announced a state-wide competition entitled "City of the Future." A large prize will be awarded to the group that creates the best design for an ideal city. The contestants should keep in mind issues that are important to any city, like public health and safety, education, the environment, transportation and economic health.

As city planners, you see this contest as a great opportunity to have an impact on future city development around the state, and beyond. Of course you would like to win the prize money, but it is more important that everyone learns about your ideas for ideal cities.

Write down your ideas for the city of the future. You will probably want to include a map and some drawings of different parts of the city.

Teacher Instructions

A Place of Our Own
Planning a Community

With "A Place of Our Own," students create a design for a "city of the future." They solve the problem of how to deal with issues like transportation and public health and safety in designing an ideal city.

Getting started

- Gather materials for making maps.
- Organize the class into groups of three to five students each. Assign the roles of *leader, scribe, presenter* and *participant*. (See box on next page.)
- Go over the problem on page 81 with the class. You may reproduce the situation as a handout or overhead transparency, or you may present it orally to the class.

Creating questions

Supervise as the class brainstorms a list of questions. Ask, "What questions need to be answered in order to plan a city?" Write the suggested questions on an overhead transparency or on the chalkboard. You may want to direct students to some of the support questions below.

Support questions:

- What will the population of the city be?
- How large will the area of the city be?
- Where will the city be? What is the landscape of this area?
- What businesses or industries will be in the city?
- What recreation facilities will be available?
- Will there be public transportation? If so, what kind?
- What issues might be of concern to the city? How will we deal with them?

Answering the questions

In their small groups, have students decide which questions they will answer in order to plan their city. Set the minimum number of questions (five or more) at a level suited to the class. Also set a time limit for this portion of the activity. Thirty to forty-five minutes is usually about right.

After the students decide on the questions, they should then write answers to them. Remind students that while the answers are fictitious, they must be realistic and appropriate for the assignment.

Copyright © 1998 Cottonwood Press, Inc. • 305 West Magnolia, Suite 398 • Fort Collins, Colorado 80521

Teacher Instructions continued

Making plans

Have students plan their cities, making maps and drawings to illustrate their plans.

During the activity

While students are working on their answers to the questions, move from group to group, making sure that all students remain active during the work time. Review the specific responsibilities of each group member the first time you check in with a group. At other check-ins, encourage students to consider the following:

- Is everyone getting a chance to talk?
- How will this question help with the organization of the city?
- Are you keeping track of the time? We have _____ minutes left.
- How will you decide where to place business and residential areas?
- Are you considering the environmental impact of your decisions?
- What groups in the community might object to this design? How can you deal with their concerns?

Reporting

When the allotted time has passed, gather all the groups together again and have the presenter from each group report to the class. The report from each group should include the questions selected, the answers given and a display of the map and drawings made by the group. If desired, the rest of the class may ask questions which any member of the reporting group may answer.

Assessing the activity

At the completion of the activity, use the "Closure Discussion" handout on page 14 to have students monitor their progress at working in small groups to solve problems.

Group Roles

Everyone in each group has an assigned role, and everyone has a responsibility to participate. The roles are:

- **Leader.** The leader is responsible for keeping the group on task, making sure all members participate and keeping track of time.

- **Scribe.** The scribe is responsible for writing down questions used and answers given, and for making any necessary charts or diagrams.

- **Presenter.** The presenter is responsible for explaining the group's activity during the reporting session.

- **Participant.** All participants have a responsibility to take part in the activity in a positive way.

Copyright © 1998 Cottonwood Press, Inc. • 305 West Magnolia, Suite 398 • Fort Collins, Colorado 80521

A Place of Our Own
Related Activities

English

- Every year, newspapers report on the "most livable" or "safest" or "healthiest" cities in the United States. Have students research one of the cities on a specific list and report on what makes it a good place to live.

Social studies

- Have students research and compare cities of similar size in different parts of the United States, reporting on the similarities and differences they find.

General

- Invite a city planner to your class to discuss his or her job and what makes your community unique.
- Have students design a mass transit system for their imaginary city.
- Have students think of ways to improve the city they actually live in. Would it be better if it had more bike paths, a new parking garage, a bigger ice-skating rink, etc.?

Art

- Have students design a logo for their city.

Total Loss
Helping Other Children

The problem to solve:

There has been a terrible flood in the city of Jefferson. Many businesses and houses were swept away by the currents of the Willihatchee River. Thousands more houses, apartments and mobile homes have been badly damaged. Although no lives were lost, the people of Jefferson have suffered greatly. They have lost a great deal of clothing, furniture and personal belongings.

Your help is urgently needed. You have been assigned to a special task force that will focus on helping the children of Jefferson. Your group is to produce a list of items to be purchased with donations. Funds are limited, so you must rank the items, putting the most urgently needed items first.

Teacher Instructions

Total Loss
Helping Other Children

With "Total Loss," students solve a problem that might be encountered by an organization in a relief effort. They must solve the problem of how to prioritize the needs of children who live in a disaster area.

Getting started

- Organize the class into groups of three to five students each. Assign the roles of *leader, scribe, presenter* and *participant*. (See box on next page.)
- Go over the problem on page 85 with the class. You may reproduce the situation as a handout or overhead transparency, or you may present it orally to the class.

Creating questions

Supervise as the class brainstorms a list of questions. Ask, "What questions need to be answered in order to make a list of items to send to the children of Jefferson?" Write the suggested questions on an overhead transparency or on the chalkboard. You may want to direct students to some of the support questions below.

Support questions:

- What are the ages of the kids we are going to help?
- What is the weather like in the city of Jefferson?
- What clothing do kids need for school? For home?
- Where are the kids staying until they can get back into their homes?
- What furniture would a family need?
- What might help the children feel better?
- What school supplies should be sent?

Answering the questions

In their small groups, have students decide which questions they will answer in order to make their list. Set the minimum number of questions (five or more) at a level suited to the class. Also set a time limit for this portion of the activity. Thirty minutes is usually about right.

After the students decide on the questions, they should then write answers to them. Remind students that while the answers are fictitious, they must be realistic and appropriate for a real emergency.

Copyright © 1998 Cottonwood Press, Inc. • 305 West Magnolia, Suite 398 • Fort Collins, Colorado 80521

Teacher Instructions continued

Making lists

Have students make their lists, ranking the items from most important to least important.

During the activity

While students are working on their answers to the questions, move from group to group, making sure that all students remain active during the work time. Review the specific responsibilities of each group member the first time you check in with a group. At other check-ins, encourage students to consider the following:

- Is everyone getting a chance to talk?
- How will this question help you decide what to send?
- Are you keeping track of the time? We have _____ minutes left.
- Are you including items that can be readily shipped to another state?
- Are you considering the prices? Remember that many children are in need.
- Why is this an important item to include?
- How will this item help the children?

Reporting

When the allotted time has passed, gather all the groups together again and have the presenter from each group report to the class. The report should include the questions selected, the answers given and the list decided upon by the group. If desired, the rest of the class may ask questions which any member of the reporting group may answer.

Assessing the activity

At the completion of the activity, use the "Closure Discussion" handout on page 14 to have students monitor their progress at working in small groups to solve problems.

Group Roles

Everyone in each group has an assigned role, and everyone has a responsibility to participate. The roles are:

- **Leader.** The leader is responsible for keeping the group on task, making sure all members participate and keeping track of time.
- **Scribe.** The scribe is responsible for writing down questions used and answers given, and for making any necessary charts or diagrams.
- **Presenter.** The presenter is responsible for explaining the group's activity during the reporting session.
- **Participant.** All participants have a responsibility to take part in the activity in a positive way.

Copyright © 1998 Cottonwood Press, Inc. • 305 West Magnolia, Suite 398 • Fort Collins, Colorado 80521

Total Loss
Related Activities

English

- Have students research and report on a recent flood or other natural disaster.
- Ask students to imagine being a TV newscaster on the scene of the floods in Jefferson. Have them write the script for their broadcast. If possible, videotape them as they use the script for a mock broadcast.

Social studies

- Have students research and report on how the government determines what constitutes a state of emergency. What, exactly, does "state of emergency" mean?
- Contact members of your city or county government to discover whether or not your community has a disaster evacuation plan for natural disasters or emergencies. Have the class make a display communicating the information in that plan.

Science

- Ask each group to research a major river in the United States or another country. Have them report on its history of flooding and efforts that have been made to control its floods.
- Have students use geology and geography resource books to make a model of a river, showing the river's normal course and the areas where flooding can occur.

General

- Have the groups research disaster relief organizations such as the Red Cross. Ask them to make a directory of these organizations, including their purpose and how to contact them.
- Invite a representative of the National Guard to class to discuss the National Guard's role in a disaster situation.

Fit for a King
Putting Together a Menu

The problem to solve:

Thanks for volunteering to work at the Good Friend Shelter. Every Friday night, this shelter provides a dinner for the homeless people in the community. Since all of you are well-known for your cooking abilities, you have been asked to plan the menu for a special five-course holiday meal next week.

You will need an appetizer, soup, salad, a main course and dessert. You will also need to include a beverage.

Be sure to use nutritious foods in ample portions. Include foods from all the food groups, and consider how the foods look as well as taste. While the budget includes extra money for this special meal, funds are not unlimited. Choose your menu carefully, with an eye to cost as well as appeal.

Teacher Instructions

Fit for a King
Putting Together a Menu

With "Fit for a King," students solve a problem that might be encountered by an organizer of a community service project. They decide what foods to include in a special holiday menu.

Getting started

- Organize the class into groups of three to five students each. Assign the roles of *leader, scribe, presenter* and *participant*. (See box on next page.)

- Go over the problem on page 89 with the class. You may reproduce the situation as a handout or overhead transparency, or you may present it orally to the class.

Creating questions

Supervise as the class brainstorms a list of questions. Ask, "What questions need to be answered in order to plan a holiday meal at a shelter?" Write the suggested questions on an overhead transparency or on the chalkboard. You may want to direct students to some of the support questions below.

Support questions:
- How many people will be served?
- What are the food groups that need to be included?
- What local dishes should be included?
- What foreign foods can be used?
- Who will do the cooking?
- How much are we allowed to spend on this meal?

Answering the questions

In their small groups, have students decide which questions they think need to be answered in order to plan the menu. Set the minimum number of questions (five or more) at a level suited to the class. Also set a time limit for this portion of the activity. Thirty minutes is usually about right.

After students decide on the questions, they should write answers to them. Remind students that while the answers are fictitious, they must be realistic and appropriate for the assignment.

Copyright © 1998 Cottonwood Press, Inc. • 305 West Magnolia, Suite 398 • Fort Collins, Colorado 80521

Teacher Instructions continued

Planning the menu

Have groups use their answers to plan the menu.

During the activity

While students are working on their answers to the questions, move from group to group, making sure that all students remain active during the work time. Review the specific responsibilities of each group member the first time you check in with a group. At other check-ins, encourage students to consider the following:

- Is everyone getting a chance to talk?
- How will this question help you decide what food to serve?
- Are you keeping track of the time? We have _____ minutes left.
- Is this a practical item to include?
- Are you considering all of the basic food groups?

Reporting

When the allotted time has passed, gather all the groups together again and have the presenter from each group report to the class. The report from each group should include the questions selected, the answers given and the menu. If desired, the rest of the class may ask questions, which any member of the reporting group may answer.

Assessing the activity

At the completion of the activity, use the "Closure Discussion" handout on page 14 to have students monitor their progress at working in small groups to solve problems.

Group Roles

Everyone in each group has an assigned role, and everyone has a responsibility to participate. The roles are:

- **Leader.** The leader is responsible for keeping the group on task, making sure all members participate and keeping track of time.

- **Scribe.** The scribe is responsible for writing down questions used and answers given, and for making any necessary charts or diagrams

- **Presenter.** The presenter is responsible for explaining the group's activity during the reporting session.

- **Participant.** All participants have a responsibility to take part in the activity in a positive way.

Copyright © 1998 Cottonwood Press, Inc. • 305 West Magnolia, Suite 398 • Fort Collins, Colorado 80521

Fit for a King
Related Activities

English

- Have students write an ad that encourages people to contribute time and/or money to the homeless shelter.

Social studies

- Ask students to choose a foreign country. Have them research and report on how the homeless are cared for there.
- Have students prepare a chart that shows cities with a high homeless population.
- Have students prepare a graph that shows the estimated number of homeless people in the United States each year for the past 20 years.

Health

- Have students use magazine pictures to make a collage of foods that illustrate the food pyramid.
- Have students research and report on malnutrition and its effects on the body.

Art

- Have students make a poster advertising Friday's special meal.

General

- Have each group research and report on a community volunteer group or governmental agency that provides assistance to people in need.
- Have the class plan and carry out a food drive for a local charity.
- Invite a social worker to your classroom to discuss the special needs of people in your community.
- Have students talk with cooks from the school cafeteria. Ask them to gather tips and other information on cooking for large numbers of people.

Math

- Set a realistic budget for serving a specified number of people at the homeless shelter. Have students make a shopping list of items to buy for the meal, adjusting the menu as necessary to stay within the budget.

Statuesque
Honoring the Past

The problem to solve:

This area needs more statues! After all, everybody knows that all the great places have statues. Athens, Paris, Buenos Aires, Tokyo — all are filled with statues of heroes, artists, writers, leaders from the past, mermaids and more. The city of Boston even has statues of a mother duck and her ducklings.

Since all of you know about this area of the country and its history, you are being given the opportunity to design at least two statues that will help represent what is important to the community. One of the statues should be of a person, living or dead. The other should capture the spirit or essence of the area, or reflect something important about the community.

Teacher Instructions

Statuesque
Honoring the Past

With "Statuesque," students design two public monuments, one memorializing a person and one capturing the spirit or essence of the area. They solve the problem of deciding what subjects will best represent what is important to the people where they live.

Getting started

- Before beginning this activity, you may want to collect books containing pictures of statues and public monuments. You may also want to gather materials for illustrating statues.
- Organize the class into groups of three to five students each. Assign the roles of *leader, scribe, presenter* and *participant*. (See box on next page.)
- Go over the problem on page 93 with the class. You may reproduce the situation as a handout or overhead transparency, or you may present it orally to the class.

Creating questions

Supervise as the class brainstorms a list of questions. Ask, "What questions need to be answered in order to design appropriate statues for our city?" Write the suggested questions on an overhead transparency or on the chalkboard. You may want to direct students to some of the support questions below.

Support questions:

- Whom shall we honor with the statue?
- What are some things about our community that should be honored with a statue?
- Where will the statues be placed?
- How large will the statues be?
- How can we represent an important event in the history of our city?
- What materials will be used to construct the statues?

Answering the questions

In their small groups, have students decide which questions they think need to be answered in order to design appropriate statues for their city. Set the minimum number of questions (five or more) at a level suited to the class. Also set a time limit for this portion of the activity. Thirty minutes is usually about right.

After the students decide on the questions, they should then write answers to them. Remind students that while the answers are fictitious, they must be realistic and appropriate for the assignment.

Copyright © 1998 Cottonwood Press, Inc. • 305 West Magnolia, Suite 398 • Fort Collins, Colorado 80521

Teacher Instructions continued

Designing statues

Have groups use their answers to design statues for the city.

During the activity

While students are working on their answers to the questions, move from group to group, making sure that all students remain active during the work time. Review the specific responsibilities of each group member the first time you check in with a group. At other check-ins, encourage students to consider the following:

- Is everyone getting a chance to talk?
- How will this question help in making decisions about the statues?
- Are you keeping track of the time? We have _____ minutes left.
- Does the design of your statue match the subject?
- What is the environmental impact of your choices?
- What does this statue "say" about your community?

Reporting

When the allotted time has passed, gather all the groups together again and have the presenters report to the class. The report from each group should include the questions selected, the answers given and the sketches of the statues. If desired, the rest of the class may ask questions which any member of the reporting group may answer.

Assessing the activity

At the completion of the activity, use the "Closure Discussion" handout on page 14 to have students monitor their progress at working in small groups to solve problems.

Group Roles

Everyone in each group has an assigned role, and everyone has a responsibility to participate. The roles are:

- **Leader.** The leader is responsible for keeping the group on task, making sure all members participate and keeping track of time.

- **Scribe.** The scribe is responsible for writing down questions used and answers given, and for making any necessary charts or diagrams

- **Presenter.** The presenter is responsible for explaining the group's activity during the reporting session.

- **Participant.** All participants have a responsibility to take part in the activity in a positive way.

Copyright © 1998 Cottonwood Press, Inc. • 305 West Magnolia, Suite 398 • Fort Collins, Colorado 80521

Statuesque
Related Activities

English

- Research and report on the building of a famous statue or monument, like the Statue of Liberty or the Vietnam Memorial.
- Write a brief biography of the person your group chose for a statue.

General

- Have students make a three dimensional model of one of the group's statues.
- Have students draw a map of the area where one of the statues will be placed.
- Have students use a map of your city or town and make suggestions about where new statues or monuments could be placed.
- Have students make a list of existing statues and monuments in your town or city, and then make a tourist directory of them.
- Have students make a tourist pamphlet about one of the statues created by your group.